Widowed.

Rants, Raves and *Randoms*

John Polo

Widowed.
Rants, Raves and *Randoms*

John Polo of Better Not Bitter Widower

Editor: Cecilia Goudanis

www.betternotbitterwidower.com

ISBN-10: 1974676978
ISBN-13: 978-1974676972

Parchment paper on pages 10, 15, 35, 41, 51, 87, 119, 135, 143, 147 designed by nuchylee / Freepik
Caligraphic border on pages 34 & 74 designed by Freepik
dearjoe4 font software is owned by JOEBOB graphics.

We may have held her up.

But in truth, it is because of her -
that we have grown.

No matter how far along in your journey you get, those moments will still come.

Those moments where your eyes fill with tears, your heart fills with sorrow, and the memories and absence take your breath away.

Those moments do not represent weakness.

Exactly the opposite.

Those are the moments in which your strength is defined.

Why We Talk About Them

We talk about them because we love them. In life. And in death.

We talk about them because they are still a part of us. And always will be.

We talk about them because the love that we shared and the loss that we endured
have shaped us into the person that we are today.

We talk about them because we find it therapeutic. For our minds. For our hearts. For our souls.

We talk about them because it helps us. And we hope that it will help others.

We talk about them because the memories make us happy. And we need to feel that.

We talk about them because the memories make us sad. And we need to feel that.

We talk about them because we want the world to know the struggle.

Of cancer. Of suicide. Of drug addiction. Of heart disease. Of sudden death. Of terminal illness.

The struggle of loss.

We talk about them because we want you to appreciate what you have.
Because in hindsight, we realize we may not have.

We talk about them because they are still ours. And we are still theirs.

We talk about them because in the day to day grind that is life, we sometimes feel them drifting away.
And we know that talking about them will make us feel closer to them today.

We talk about them because we want to.

We talk about them because we need to.

And yes, sometimes, we talk about them because nobody else is.

It is now our responsibility to carry on their legacies.

We talk about them because we take that responsibility very seriously.

When Michelle was sick and dying, she would often tell me of her fears that everyone would forget her.
That she would become a distant memory. That nobody would speak of her anymore.
That it would be like she never existed.

Nope. Not going to happen. Not on my watch. Not now. Not ever.

We talk about them because we refuse to let them be forgotten.

Anybody who says this to you is a

JACKASS.

" Get over it already. "

Widowed. Rants, Raves and *Randoms*

Love Is

Love is, You.

Love is, Me.

Love Is, We.

Love is, John.

Love is, Michelle.

Love is, Heaven.

Love is, Hell.

Love is, the Greatest Spell.

Love is, Body to Body.

Love is, Soul to Soul.

Love is, What Picks You Up After the Fall.

Love is, It All.

Love is, Bliss.

Love is, Each and Every Kiss.

Love is, Moments Shared.

Love is, How Much We Cared.

Love is, Sickness.

Love is, Health.

Love is, The Greatest Wealth.

Love is, All of the Tears.

Love is, Persistence Through All of the Fears.

Love is, Heart.

Love is, Not Even Death Could Tear us Apart.

Cecilia and Sam

Widowed. Rants, Raves and *Randoms*

Meet Cecilia

Cecilia was married to the love of her life, Sam.

5 ½ years into their love, Sam passed away at the age of 24 from heart failure.

Sam and Cecilia were married a very short time in calendar years,
but in meaning and purpose, they shared a lifetime together.

Here is a Facebook post that Cecilia made:

 Cecilia

All of the monthly anniversaries that have come and gone since Sam passed have made me incredibly sad. How could they not? We were given less than 5 months of marriage. We were robbed of experiences married couples typically get to have. Grief is a funny and unpredictable thing, though. Today, on what would be our 9-month wedding anniversary, I'm smiling because I'm grateful for the months we did have as a married couple, and the years before that. I'm blessed that I know that marriage isn't all fun and games. It's filled with unconditional and selfless love. It involves taking care of your spouse in ways you never imagined you would have to. It includes making decisions you never thought you would have to make. It becomes watching your spouse's physical, mental, and emotional health deteriorate daily and realizing what's ahead, but never letting him see your fear. It's dirty and hard work, but it's one of the most honorable jobs. I miss this man every single day and always will, but at least for today, I'm going to smile and remember the memories we shared and the adventures we took together. I'm going to feel incredibly thankful that I was chosen to be a part of his journey. I'm going to feel lucky that I experienced a kind of love that not many get to have. I'm going to feel humbled that he held on long enough for me to arrive before he left, and that I could make him feel comfortable enough to let go.

I was that for someone.

How amazing is that?

How can I not smile?

Cecilia. She inspires me.

Sneak Peek of My Upcoming Book

My Michelle

That's all that it took - one phone call and Michelle and I were truly connected again. We had graduated from the e-mail version of our newfound friendship and now needed more. We needed to talk, we needed to hear each other's voices and laughs. Days would turn into weeks and we would text, and we would talk almost every day - still mostly about generic stuff - until one day, we pressed hard on the gas, accelerating our relationship to a place we both wanted to exist but were, for a long time now, too scared to go.

"Do you ever think about us?" she asked.

I hope I live a long life.

I want to help others. I want to fall in love again.

I want to be the best step-dad that I can be.

I want to enjoy grand kids.

BUT...

When it's my time,

I'm sprinting up there.

Sprinting.

Forrest Gump style.

#To #See #Her

Have it Ready for Me

February 6, 2016:

This was supposed to be our wedding day.

A day that we would erase the memory of our actual wedding day, July 26, 2013; a day in which we were married at a courthouse. Michelle was violently ill that day, in extreme pain and throwing up non-stop.

It was 4 days after her cancer diagnosis.

5 days before her 8-hour surgery was scheduled to take place.

February 6, 2016:

We had it all planned.

The Ivy Hotel.

Downtown Chicago.

This was the day that I would finally get to watch the love of my life walk down the aisle.

Something that I had dreamt about since I fell in love with her, at the young age of 18.

We never got our dream wedding, but one day we will.

When it's my time, whenever that may be - here is my request.

Michelle,

Have it all ready for me.

All of it. Perfectly. Just as we had imagined.

Have the dress on, that beautiful dress that you loved so much.
I never got to see you in it, but I know that I will.
The gorgeous shoes that you looked like an absolute princess in.
The hair, the makeup, all of it.

Have the candles and the flowers and our colors, purple and grey.

Have the special chairs that we were supposed to leave unattended to honor
Michael, Kevin, Rose and Nicole.

Have Etta.

But don't have her on a speaker system. No, instead have her there with you.

Have her sing. That song.

That song that told our story so perfectly. That song that you were supposed to walk down the aisle to.

"At Last" by Etta James.

A song that I have loved forever and suggested you walk down to. And after hearing it, you agreed.

Have it all ready for me.

My grey suit and purple bow tie.

The aisle.

Etta singing.

You walking down.

That smile. Those lips.

Those vows. That kiss.

Do you know what widows and widowers miss?

Everything.

We miss everything.

The good.

The bad.

Yes.

We miss it all.

Sneak Peek of My Upcoming Book

My Michelle

No way was I going to call her first. Nope, was not going to happen! It was noon and I had made my mind up. I would play hardball with her and there would be no communication until she reached out to me. If that took another couple days, or a week or a month, so be it! I was going to be tough.

At 6:30pm, I decided to call her.

Yes. I buckled.

LaTisha

Widowed. Rants, Raves and *Randoms*

Meet LaTisha

I have never met LaTisha in "real life," only via the virtual world.

Even though we have never met, I can tell that there is something amazing about her spirit.
It shines.

LaTisha lost her husband, Andre, to suicide.

I have come to learn from others in the grieving community that loss via suicide
carries with it a very difficult and unique type of grief.

It has not been an easy journey for LaTisha, but she is not only surviving – no, she is thriving.

Here is a Facebook post that LaTisha made:

 LaTisha

This week is usually rough for me.

Saturday will be 6 years since my late husband took his own life. But I have a joy in my heart of moving forward that I cannot explain. 6 years ago, I could not answer the question, "Where do you see yourself in 5 years?" I could not even see past the current day. Are things perfect? Not in the least. But I have peace and joy, a new path and a new direction. I see a future for my children and me, and although, unfortunately, it does not include their dad, various other people we have lost contact with along the way, or at this point even a Chapter 2…

What it DOES include is US!

What it DOES include is ME!

LaTisha. She inspires me.

**For the first few months after her passing,
I slept with Michelle's urn next to my bed.**

I would give her (it) a good-night kiss each evening before I went to sleep.

One night, it turned into a make out session.

Yes, I made out with my wife's urn.

In fairness, it was only for about 10 seconds.

But still, it happened.

Do you think I am weird?

Good.

I don't care.

#grief

#do #not #judge

#I #lost #my #love

Better Not Bitter Widower Facebook Post

better
not bitter widower

No matter how strong you try to be, true grief will always have its moments.

For me, it was a 20-minute breakdown today.

Tears coming down, sounding like some kind of high-pitched animal because this cry was from the gut.

Moments like this are when I miss Michelle the most.

My best friend.

But it stopped.

And life continues.

And somehow, you get through the day.

Because tomorrow might be better.

And because you can get through this.

Even though at moments, it seems impossible.

If She Were My Widow

Michelle,

It's National Widows Day. May 3rd.

I know you don't pay a lot of attention to these types of things.

But I also know you heard.

I see you cry. Every single day.

It hurts me still.

I wish there was another way.

You know I fought so hard.

With all of my might.

I didn't want to stop.

You and your daughter.

Both worth the fight.

My body was tired.

My mind so weak.

I had to stop fighting Michelle.

There was no cure to seek.

I want you to know, that you were always the one.

My love for you never went away.

It still hasn't.

It never will.

By the way, the baby we lost.

I have him.

Yes. A son.

He looks just like you.

Thank goodness for that.

Although he has my cheeks.

Nice and fat.

I know you feel alone.

You're sad and scared.

You cry out to God angrily, and ask him why I could not be spared.

The answers you are looking for, won't come to you now.

Just know that eventually, you will see why, and you will see how.

I want you to know that I was there at hospice.

Through the sleep, I saw.

What you did for me.

The tears.

The love.

That was pure.

That was raw.

I heard the eulogy that you read to me.

Yes, I listened.

Yes, I saw.

I love you so much.

I always will.

You are my soul mate.

Past, future and still.

You can do this Michelle.

You are stronger than you know.

Happiness. Not survival.

That should be the goal.

Our love is more than that world.

It's soul to soul.

It is okay to be angry. It is okay to be bitter.

These are normal, human emotions that one is expected to have after dealing with a profound loss.

Believe me, I know. Believe me, I understand.

I was as bitter as bitter could be.

In order to make any progress in your journey of healing, you must honor these feelings.

Just don't live there forever.

Ultimately, each and every one of us must make a decision.

We can allow the anger and bitterness to eat away at our minds,
our hearts and our souls for the rest of time,

OR…

We can experience these emotions, and in time, we can work our way through them.

Better.

Not Bitter.

No. It is not easy.

Yes. It is possible.

There will come a time when you catch yourself smiling again.

There will come a time when you catch yourself laughing again.

There will come a time when you catch yourself enjoying a moment of happiness again.

You may feel guilty.

Do. Not. Feel. Guilty.

My wife was obsessed with her own feet.

I would catch her staring at them all of the time with a big smile on her face.

"They're just so pretty," she would say.

#she #was #so #weird

#don't #tell #her #i #told #you

Counseling/Therapy 101

Some say they don't want counseling. Some say they don't need counseling.
That's fine, but personally speaking, I am a big believer in counseling. In bereavement.

In seeking some sort of help. Some sort of support. Some sort of release.

When you lose a loved one, your life is turned upside-down.
Your mind is tired. Your heart is broken.
Help is available. Help can be sought.

As a couple, Michelle and I sought counseling toward the end of her cancer battle.
As an individual, I sought counseling during her cancer battle. Often.
I had to cry to someone. I had to vent to someone. I had to let it out.
The pain, the agony - it was too much to bear alone.
The realization of what was soon to come was eating away at my insides,
and I knew that I could not fight such a battle on my own.

Those that I sought out listened to my pain and my fears,
they acknowledged my raw emotion, and they aided me.
Working with them helped me emotionally, to let it all out.
Working with them helped me mentally, by helping me to understand
my emotions and the emotions of those around me.
They helped me to be a better husband to my dying wife,
a better step-father to our broken-hearted little girl,
and a better overall me.

To this day, I still seek counseling.
I seek one-on-one counseling, and I seek group counseling.
Both are helpful in their own unique ways.

You do not need to go at this alone.
Help is available.
It has helped me.
I believe it can help you, too.

#there #is #no #weakness

#in #seeking #help

"It's been 17 months," they said.

"But she's still dead," I said.

Sit Down. And Shut Up.

Sit down.

And shut up.

Serious question: Is your spouse 6 feet under? Oh wait, are they a pile of ashes?

No?

They aren't?

Wow.

Okay.

Cool.

Then, sit down.

And shut up.

My wife's name was Michelle. She's gone.

Once a widow. Always a widow.

Once a widower. Always a widower.

No, this is not a plea for sympathy.

No, these are not angry words.

These are honest words.

These are passionate words.

These are real words.

Sit down.

And shut up.

Unless you watched your spouse die. Unless you buried your spouse. Unless you burned your spouse.

Sit down.

And shut up.

Do not tell a widow or widower how they should be living.

Do not tell a widow or widower how they should be acting.

And please, for the love of all that is right in this world, PLEASE do NOT tell a widow or widower when they should try to love again.

I am sick of seeing widows and widowers vilified for trying to pick up the pieces of their lives.

I am sick of seeing widows and widowers vilified for trying to find companionship again.

For trying to find love again.

Hell, for trying to find ANYTHING again!

We are lost souls. On a journey to find our self again.

And YOU want to judge?

You?

Do you know the courage it takes to go back out there after your spouse has died?

After you watched them die of cancer. Or a massive heart attack. Or suicide.

After you watched them fall to 60 pounds. Having bowel movements on themselves. Having horrific hallucinations so bad that seeing them like that strangled your soul.

After you watched them fall to their knees. And clutch their chest. And take their last breath.

After you walked in on their body. Dead. Because they took their own life.

You have no idea.

Do you have any idea how badly the loss of a spouse messes with your mind? With your heart? With your soul?

No. You don't.

So, sit down.

And shut up.

You are not allowed to judge.

You are not allowed to pass judgment as you drive home to your spouse.

You are not allowed to pass judgment as you eat dinner with your spouse.

You are not allowed to pass judgment as you cuddle up on the couch with your spouse.

You are not allowed to pass judgment as you have sexy time with your spouse.

You. Are. Not. Allowed. To. Pass. Judgment.

Sit down.

And shut up.

Stop judging.

Stop thinking that you know what the Hell you are talking about.

Because you do not.

Your life wasn't ripped from you.

Your future wasn't destroyed.

Sit down.

And shut up.

This was not our choice.

This was not a breakup. Stop comparing.

This was not a divorce. Stop comparing.

This was not the loss of a grandpa. Stop comparing.

This was not the loss of Uncle Thomas. Stop comparing.

And, for Heaven's sake, this was NOT the loss of your damn CAT. Stop comparing!

This was the loss of a soul mate.

Our other half.

Our life.

Our love.

Our future.

Sit down.

And shut up.

The next time you see a widow or widower try to pick themselves off, dust themselves off and 'Get back out there'....

You have 2 choices.

You can either sit down and shut up,

Or...

You can give them a standing ovation.

For their heart. For their courage. For their bravery.

Those are your 2 options.

And your ONLY 2 options.

Because. You. Do. Not. Know.

- Rant. Over. -

Mic Drop.

Memories fade.

Consider making a memory book.

Customize the front cover.

Then have family and friends write down their favorite memories or thoughts about your late spouse, and you do the same.

Include pictures as well, and caption them.

This is a great way to preserve as many memories as possible, and is especially important if you have young children.

This can also be a very therapeutic activity.

They Say...

"So, for now, I cling to the memories. I look for the signs. I cry and scream and yell and yearn to fell his presence around me. Because loving someone is equally the most wonderful and most painful thing I have ever done." - Emily Ann

"There is a wedding photo in our house. I talk to it often knowing that it will bring me to tears, but I do it anyway. Sadness is often the only contact I have." - Kevin

"Sometimes my girls catch me staring at them and smiling. They ask me why, and I tell them because I see their daddy living in them. They smile back at me proudly, knowing that it's true. The truth is I am a better person because he died. I am sad that it took his death to open my eyes. He showed me what's important in life, because tomorrow is not guartneed." - Jen

"When Walter died so suddenly, I thought my world ended with him that cold January evening. Yet, I am still here. I loved him before he died, but now that love has become so intense that it is over-flowing. What do I do with so much love?" – Alina

#idontusehashtagsthewrongway

#you #use #hashtags #the #wrong #way

Say. Their. Name.

#Widowed #Strong

We CAN grieve as we move forward.

We CAN move forward as we grieve.

The two ideas are NOT mutually exclusive.

They can walk hand in hand.

Sneak Peek of My Upcoming Book

My Michelle

Michelle and I lost our way with each other and started our own, separate lives.

I would think about her often the first couple of years but, eventually,

I tried to block her out of my mind. It hurt too much.

What I would come to find out years later, though, is that true love never dies.

You can try and hide it, not think about it, stuff it somewhere deep inside your heart,

deep inside your mind and your soul to a place you rarely visit,

but it never truly goes away.

The Brick

By Tim

One afternoon, I was out for a walk on my break at the college that I work at.
I was minding my own business until I crossed the courtyard and out of the corner
of my eye I saw the brick. It was the brick that my wife Roberta and I had written our
names and date of marriage on. We had donated money to have that brick.
I bent down and traced my finger on her name and started crying my eyes out.

Eventually, I gathered myself and walked into one of the departments at the college.

I thought that I had pulled myself together completely, but all it took was the secretary to
ask if I was alright and that did it. I sat down in the chair next to her desk
and started crying my eyes out again, this time in an office full of people.

She did exactly what you want someone to do in this type of situation
(most people try to stop you).
She stood up and put her hand on my shoulder and said that it was okay,
and to let it out.

That's all you really want, someone to understand
and to not make you feel bad for losing it.

On that day, the brick did me in.

I love you, Michelle!

#Always #Have

#Always #Will

Many widows and widowers suffer from anxiety and panic attacks.

I know I do.

Here are some options to consider:

Yoga, Meditation, Daily Exercise.

Breathing exercises can help as well.

Take a deep, slow breath for 7 seconds.

Now, exhale for 7 seconds.

#rinse & #repeat

It always amazes me whenever I receive a message from someone telling me how much my words have meant to them.

It usually happens around 7:00pm.

As I lay in bed.

In my underwear.

Stuffing my face with Doritos.

#nacho #cheese #are #my #favorite

#cool #ranch #are #good #too #tho

Michelle

#da #wifey

She was the most beautiful person I've ever known.

Inside & Out.

Excerpt from Better Not Bitter Widower Blog

"The Cancer Survivor, Redefined"

My wife may no longer be here.

Cancer may have forced her Home.

But, my wife survived cancer.

Michelle survived cancer because of how she fought.
Brave as could be.

Michelle survived cancer because of how she lived.
Full of love.

Michelle survived cancer because of how she smiled.
Genuinely, and up until the very end.

Michelle survived cancer because of the memories and enduring legacy
that she leaves behind.

She will never be forgotten.

Anxiety/Depression/PTSD

If you think you may be suffering from any, or all of these, talk to your doctor.

#No #Shame

No perfect combination of words is going to fix the situation, or mend a broken heart.

So many run from the grieving because they feel as though they don't know how to fix things, or even make them better.

The thing is, nobody asked them to fix things.

Nobody asked them to make them better.

Some days, when it seems like the absence of our lost love is too much to bear, it's not the words or actions that help us get through the moments, or the day.

It's the presence.

The presence of a caring soul.

#Just #Be #There

I used to sing and dance for Michelle all of the time.

Mind you, when I say "for Michelle," I mean to torment her.

#Yes

#It's #That #Bad

#I #Think #She #Secretely #Liked #It #Though

#I #Got #Moves

I know you are sad.

I know you are lonely.

I know.

BUT…

That is not an excuse to settle for someone who does not treat you the right way.

You are a Rockstar.

You have overcome the unthinkable.

You deserve the best.

Accept nothing less.

#Love #Yourself

Thank You, Sam

Sam was so full of love. Whether for me, his family, friends, strangers, or animals, there was so much love that he gave to this world. His laugh was contagious, he went out of his way to make others happy and laugh (even though his sense of humor often left much to be desired), his hugs made me melt, and his compassion for others was admirable. I have always had a big heart and loved deeply, but knowing Sam opened my heart even more. Loving him was the most incredible thing I've ever experienced, and losing him was the most horrible. But, even in death, Sam has found a way to continue to bring love and happiness into my life. There are smiles on my face and room in my heart. That being said, I didn't want to date. I didn't plan on dating. I wanted to wait quite a while and find myself again. I was with Sam for 5½ years and didn't know who I was after losing him. I wanted to travel. I wanted to focus on my business. I wanted to grieve. I did those things alone for 4 months (which, when grieving, truly feels like so much longer, and I was also grieving and hurting when he was sick for those months) and then, unexpectedly and completely out of nowhere, came Aleric. Dinner and drinks with a friend turned into wanting to spend more time together and then something strange: feelings for someone for reasons other than wanting a friendship. I was afraid that I was going to regret it or find things to pick apart because he isn't Sam. But, I didn't. I still haven't. No one will ever be Sam, and that is okay. I don't want another Sam; he was one of a kind. I've realized that being with someone else doesn't replace Sam. It doesn't change the fact that I'm grieving. Also, I've realized that I don't need to validate or explain anything to anyone if I don't feel it's necessary. Even in death, he will always be a part of my life. What's important is that somehow, through all of this hurt, I've smiled. And I know deep in my heart that Sam is responsible for that.

Thank you, Sam. Thank you for showing me what love is. Thank you for loving me unconditionally and for letting me love you. Thank you for putting someone in my life that is a good fit for me, respects me, understands that I'm hurting, and comforts me, because I know you had the highest standards and wouldn't accept anything less.

Xo - Cecilia

They Ask:

"How are you?"

You Answer:

"I'm fine."

Liar.

#I #Know

It is OKAY

to not be OKAY!

There will be times in which you cry so hard that your insides begin to physically ache.

As my step-daughter once said to me while rubbing my back

"Let it out, Johnny. Just let it all out."

#tears #can #be #healing

#let #them #flow

Alicia

This is Alicia

Alicia became a widow when her husband, David, passed away of cancer at the age of 38.

Alicia is a widow.

Alicia is a single mom.

Alicia is, herself, a cancer survivor.

This is Alicia.

This is courage.

Try This, Or That

Simply declining an offer for company can sometimes lead others to be scared away.
They may not understand your changing moods, emotions and needs; therefore,
they just assume that you always want to be left alone.

Instead of simply declining such an offer, try this response instead:

"Thanks for the offer. I am not really up for it today, but I know that throughout this journey,
I am going to need a lot of continued support, so let's please plan on getting together another day."

Generally speaking, people want to help, but don't know how.

Be direct.

"It would really help me if we could go out for coffee this weekend.
I've been in the house all week and the walls feel like they are closing in."

The holidays are very hard and fairly unpredictable. You might make plans, get there,
and then want nothing more than to just go home. Or you might decide to stay home,
but then at the last minute, you desperately feel the need to be around others.

Be upfront with family and friends.

"I've decided I'm going to come for Thanksgiving, but it's been rough lately,
so I may not stay long. I need to see how I feel."

OR...

"I've decided I'm going to stay home for Christmas, but I might end up changing my mind
and needing company. Can you save a place for me around the table just in case?"

Sneak Peek of My Upcoming Book

My Michelle

I could not even let the future prospects of the cancer
returning affect me at that moment.
My wife had done it. She had defeated the beast inside of her.
Together, we would grow old. 50 beautiful years awaited us.

About an hour later, they allowed me to go back into
the recovery room while the rest of the family remained seated in the
waiting area.

I took Michelle's hand and held it so tight, kissing it over
and over again. Repeatedly I would tell her that I loved her, even though
she was sound asleep and likely
could not hear the words spoken.

Michelle's face was swollen as could be.
She looked as though she had just been beaten up in a
heavyweight boxing match.

Yet, despite all that, I had never seen her so beautiful in all of the years
that I had known her.
The feeling of pride that this woman was my wife was like nothing I had
ever felt before.
It was profound, in a completely indescribable way.

My wife. My wife. My wife.

I was beaming, from ear to ear.

They Say...

"I hate seeing other couples hold hands. I'm sorry, I know that I shouldn't, but I do. It hurts me each and every time. I hate it." - Samantha

"Grant and I were married for 27 years. A few months after he passed away, I found a love letter that he wrote me on our computer. In it, he reminded me that I should always cherish the good memories, because they far outweigh the bads one we had while he was sick. I cherish those good memories every second of every day." - Lynne

"I don't fit where I once did. I struggle being around people who are happy. I struggle connecting with people who have never experienced a devastating loss. Not that I wish sadness or loss on anybody. In fact, I wish I could go back to those happy, carefree days myself." - Emily Ann

"I feel like my grief is so much different than everyone else's. I was abused by my husband for 14 years. I miss him, but I don't have the fond memories to speak of like everyone else does. It adds to my devastation." - Jennifer

From this point on, every time someone asks you for your emergency contact, you are going to want to cry.

This is one of the most dreadful questions that the members of our unlucky club can be asked.

It feels like a kick in the gut.

Each and every time.

Answer the question the best way that you can.

After you have pulled yourself back together, purchase a boat-load of chocolate and stuff your face until you are so full that you cannot move.

Fall asleep.

When you wake up, eat more chocolate.

And tacos.

#We #Like #Tacos

The grieving community, as a whole, is very hard on itself.

It's understandable.

You've lost a piece of our heart.

But…

You're still here.

Still surviving. Still holding onto hope.

For a better tomorrow.

Give yourself a pat on the back.

If you're not proud of yourself, be proud of yourself.

I'm proud of you.

Better Not Bitter Widower Facebook Post

better not bitter widower

Whenever I feel sad, I think about the fact that I was married to Michelle.

I got to be married to her.

The girl that I fell in love with as a teenager.

8 years apart, but always in my heart.

The woman I so proudly called my wife.

The mother to the little girl that I love as my own.

I think about that.

And I smile.

Because that's pretty damn special.

A fly keeps attacking my face.

I'm tired today and don't have the energy to wave him off of me.

At first, it was flattering.

But now it's getting annoying.

This widowed life is lonely.

It's really lonely.

The Solitude that Follows

Cousins. Aunts. Uncles. Grandparents. Friends. Friends of the Family.

Dad.

Wife.

I've known loss. If you are reading this, chances are, you have, too.

For all the many, many wakes and funerals I have been to, one thing has continuously occurred to me. The wake is so much easier than the funeral.

When I sit back and think about why that is I can only come to one conclusion: Support.

There is so much support at a wake. At least in my circle of love, they usually last over 6 hours and the room is almost always filled to near-capacity. In the case of my beautiful wife, we had every seat full and another 60 people or so standing. Over 200 people attended her services on that cold January day. A full house of standing room only for a beautiful soul that certainly deserved such a fitting goodbye. People came in droves, as I stood by the casket and welcomed everyone, something that I also did at my dad's wake. With each person that came up to say their final goodbyes to Michelle, stories and memories were shared, kind and inspiring words were spoken. A sense of hope and love in a moment filled with heartache and despair.

For Michelle's wake, I opened the floor so that anyone who wanted to speak, could. After the last person who wanted to speak did, I gave the eulogy. I thought that I would cry during it, but I didn't shed a single tear as I read it. A product most likely of having read it so many times before, most notably to Michelle as she lay in a coma the morning of the day that she passed. Talk about some hardcore tears. Professing my love to her with the eulogy that I tried so hard to perfect as she lay dying.

After I was done speaking at the wake, we played 6 songs that meant so much to me and Michelle. A few from the wedding ceremony we didn't quite make it to, and a few others as well.

The wake. A moment of support, community and love.

As is always the case, the funeral the next day was attended by far less; however, the support was still there. We attended an absolutely beautiful church, played some amazing songs, including "Amazing Grace," and went to lunch with everyone after. The most beautiful moment was when my sister's father-in-law sang "Somewhere Over the Rainbow" as the pall bearers carried her light casket to the hearse. The clouds and grey suddenly making way for the sun to shine at that exact moment and, no, I'm not making that up.

And then, the funeral ends. And when all of the final good-byes are said and all of the supportive Facebook messages are sorted through and responded to, something interesting happens.

Solitude begins.

Although, in fairness, it's not complete solitude right away. Family and friends realizing the scope of loss and the rawness of it all reach out, come around, and are generally there for you.

But then, something funny happens. Some time passes. And the solitude grows.

And then, it grows some more.

And then, by the time you realize it, it's almost complete solitude.

Now, before I go on, let me state clearly: Part of this story is about me, but do not think that I am alone in this. Whether it be the in-person support groups that I go to, or one of the number of support groups I am a part of on Facebook, the undeniable fact is that the most complained about feature of being a widow or widower that I hear is this: Solitude. Or, to put in terms that I don't like to use because it makes many of us feel rather pathetic: Loneliness.

So, solitude is there and then it grows, and a part of you begins to wonder "Why?"
But then, something funny happens. You realize you are guilty of the same.

You think back and you realize that when your aunt lost both her husband and her daughter in the span of one calendar year, you told her at the funerals that you would be there for her, but you weren't. Nope, not even a little bit. You ask yourself how you could have failed a loved one like that, and you feel guilty.

But the answer is clear: For you, life moves on.

For the world, even those who love the deceased, the Earth continues to rotate, the sun continues to shine, rainy days continue to damper outdoor plans, and life moves on.

But for a select few, the loss is more profound.

And for those select few, solitude is almost certainly to follow.

"It seems like everyone avoids me."

"All my friends are married."

"I think they don't know how to act around me."

"Everyone thinks I'm fine now."

"Nobody gets it."

"People go on with their life; yours is the one forever changed."

These are some of the comments I hear or read. Over and over again. From widows and widowers who feel as though the loss of their love was simply the first step of loss in a whole new world.

Okay, it happens. We've all done it. Certainly nobody means any harm. Life goes on. I get it. We all get it.

You adjust and adapt through the grief. You try to move forward, not on.

But how?

"I just don't want to bother people."

"I don't want someone to spend time with me out of pity."

"I'm no fun anymore. I don't want to bring people down."

These are some of the comments I hear or read. Over and over again. You see, with the loss of your love, something else happens. Self-doubt.

Often, it is not immediate, but rather later in the game. Think about it. The person who was your biggest cheerleader, the person who chose you instead of anyone else in the world to spend the rest of their life with, is no longer around.

The love you felt from them is gone.

And then, slowly, other support starts to drift. And solitude grows.

And knowing that you aren't exactly the same person as you use to be, you start to feel like a burden.

And then, you take a step back, and you wonder if you are handling things correctly.

But really, what is the correct way to handle the loss of the love of your life?

Do you post about it on Facebook? Start a blog?

"Attention! Attention! He wants attention!" many will say.

"God, he needs to get over it already," others will insist.

Maybe you take the opposite approach. Maybe you act like all is okay.
Shoot, maybe you decide you want to find love again.

"If he's already looking to date, he must not have loved her that much." Yes, some will think it.

"He seems to be doing great. I don't think I would be doing that well if my spouse died," others will proclaim.

Judgment of your actions, your life, how much you laugh or don't laugh, how much you cry or don't cry begin to run rampant.

And you let it affect you. Even though you know you shouldn't.

You take it, and you internalize it because, after all,
your other half isn't there to share those feelings with anymore.

You have a lot of free time on your hands now to sit, to stir, and to think.

It used to be when something good happened, you couldn't wait to get home to tell your love.

Or, when something bad happened, you knew you would have your other half there
to help you get through it.

I mean, sure, you could text a friend or a family member.

But there's that self-doubt again.

Do you really want to be a burden to them?

"Haven't they had enough of me and my loss and my problems?" you ask yourself.

And then, Saturday comes, and after having a really good week, you all of a sudden are having a
horrible morning. You thought you were beyond this type of breakdown, but then you remember the
big-headed guy's blog from Illinois who you follow and he told you that grief comes in waves.
So, the tears are there, and they are rampant. The type of tears that make your stomach hurt.
But nobody is around to see. And you actually consider walking to a neighbor's house for a
human-to-human experience, but you don't. You get through it yourself.

"How are you today? Maybe we can do something later?" a friend of yours asks
via text messages shortly after you gather yourself.

"I'm fine. I'm not feeling well, though, so I'm going to stay in," you respond. You've learned by now
saying "I'm fine" is a lot easier than explaining why you may not be fine on that particular day.

Solitude.

And so, the cycle continues. Because, quite honestly, half of the time, you really don't want to do
anything, and the other half of the time, you don't have anything to do. And sometimes, you want to
be around certain people. And other times, you don't want to be around those same exact people.

And let's face it, sometimes being around people brings comfort, and other times,
it flashes a bright light on the void that is.

That's okay. And that's normal.

Solitude. It can be a lonely road. It can also be a two-way street.

I'm the type of parent who takes his child to the exact spot where her mom and I first made out in 2002. I tell her exactly why we are standing there as she stares at me in pure disgust.

Then, I reenact the memory using my hand.

This is who I am.

As a person.

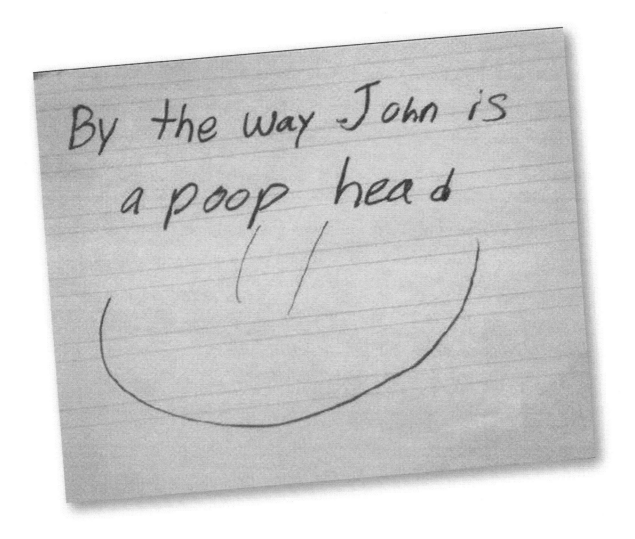

Widowed. Rants, Raves and *Randoms*

Michelle.

Again.

#Look #at #Her

#OMG

#Jaw #Dropping

#I #Know

The only thing more beautiful
than her face.

Was her soul.

They Say...

"Physical touch. Those doors slammed shut in an instant. The morning hug, the evening kiss, the hand hold, the foot massage, the hair comb, the playful carry, the sexual intimacy, the hundreds of casual touches received without a thought— all of that was yanked away. I was left grasping for anchors in a sea of nothingness." – Susan

"Do you know what it looks like to crush someone's soul? I do. I saw it on my four children's faces when I told them that their father died. It haunts me to this day. When Jeremy died, he took my smile and my laugh with him, but I am determined to not let his death kill me." – Cristy

"Dwight was the one I've loved since I was seven years old. The man I dreamt of marrying for decades of my life. He was taken a month before we would have become man and wife. He was my best friend. My wild-eyed, Beatles singing, beautiful-souled, firefly-chasing, love of my life. I'll move forward with time, but part of me rests with him forever." – Renate

"My husband killed himself. At first I told my kids that their father had a heart attack, as I didn't want them to know the truth. Now I have a different perspective. I don't blame him anymore. He tried to hold on for us for so long, but his mental illness was too much to bear." – Rosie Ann

Your grief is likely to make other people feel uncomfortable.

TOO DAMN BAD.

DO NOT

hold your nose at those who lost their spouses to suicide or drug addiction.

Just do not.

You do not know their struggles.

Less judging.

More loving.

The first time that I cuddled with a woman after Michelle's passing, I cried.

Yes. I cried.

#embarrassing #i #know

If, and when, you journey back out into the world of dating, expect the unexpected.

#there #were #a #lot #of #tears

William

Meet William

William lost his beautiful wife, Faye, to cancer.

Losing the love of your life is hard enough, but finding yourself a single father to 3 grieving children is a challenge very few of us can even imagine.

Something amazing caught my attention about William, though.

In every picture, he smiled.

With a broken heart and an uncertain future, he chose to live.

For his children. For himself. And, yes, for her.

Here is a Facebook post that William made:

 William

It's been one month since my beloved wife departed from this Earth to a perfect world. This has been the longest month of my life and I really can't believe it has only been a month. So many memories, emotions, and adjustments. I miss her more than words can describe, but I truly know that she is still with me. I can feel her every day. I find comfort in her no longer being affected by the effects of cancer and the drugs. I can also see her every day in our 3 precious children.

I want to thank everyone who has been part of this journey.

I have felt love by your words and actions that is beyond appreciation.

Here is to month two.

William. He inspires me.

In order to heal.

You must feel.

#Honor #the #Pain

There are times when I want to talk about Michelle.

There are times when I need to talk about Michelle.

And then, there are times when I absolutely cannot and do not want to talk or hear about Michelle.

Each day is unique.

Each moment, its own.

Honor your feelings.

As confusing, and scattered, as they may be.

It Bothers Me When

It Bothers Me When: I get introduced to someone as John. And there is no Michelle. That, in itself, is a moment of Hell.

It Bothers Me When: They think that I am a single man. Because I am not. I was wed. And she is dead.

It Bothers Me When: Monday. And Tuesday. Who am I kidding. It's the rest of the week too. Her absence is felt. In everything that I do.

It Bothers Me When: Happy couples. And their normal life. I can't describe. Just how much I miss my wife.

It Bothers Me When: Holidays. When she is not there. Such a harsh reality. It doesn't seem fair.

It Bothers Me When: The sun is out. Or rain is there. When snow fills the ground. No matter what the weather. The world feels bare.

It Bothers Me When: I think of the past. The love that we shared. I pleaded with God. To let her be spared.

It Bothers Me When: People judge our pain. They think we are weak. Their ignorance. A disgraceful shame.

It Bothers Me When: Fifty years. That is what is was supposed to be. I loved her so much. And she so loved me.

It Bothers Me When: EVERY DAY. Yes. The good ones too. I only wish good for people. But you'll never understand. Unless it happens to you.

About to get my guacamole on.

Not that you asked.

I just thought you'd like to know.

Grief is not weak.

Or weird.

Grief is not shameful.

Or embarrassing.

Grief is real.

And raw.

Grief is necessary.

And unstoppable.

Grief, is love.

Never let someone – especially someone who has never endured a similar loss – tell you how or what you should, or should not, be feeling.

This is your journey. Your loss. Your grief.

If need be, quote him.

Quote Uncle Willie.

#Do #You

"Well, everyone can master a grief
but he that has it."

~ William Shakespeare

Writing can be VERY therapeutic.

My suggestion would be to simply pick up a pen and a piece of paper and write down whatever comes to you.

You might be very surprised at what comes out.

Anger. Appreciation. Fear. Gratitude.

Feelings, emotions, and thoughts that you didn't even know you had may pour onto the paper effortlessly.

Specific Exercises to Try:

- Write a letter to your late spouse.
- Write a letter to yourself, as though your late spouse was writing it to you.
- Write a letter to the disease or incident that took the life of your late spouse
  (for instance, a "Dear Cancer" letter).

Kid-Friendly Idea:

- If you have children, consider creating a "Letters to Heaven" box.
- Decorate it in a fun way, perhaps with pictures, etc.
- Your children can then write letters to their Mommy or Daddy in Heaven and place them in the **box.** *This can be a good grieving tool for children, or even adults.*

I have a published journal out with twenty-two writing prompts that some of you may find helpful

Yes, They Did!

"I missed him so much. Since I couldn't have him touch me, I put some of his ashes in my body lotion. At least for the moment, I felt closer to him." - Lace

"After she passed away, I used my wife's toothbrush for the first 3 months in an effort to feel closer to her. I told my dentist (who is an old friend of mine), and he said that I was disgusting, but I didn't care." – Charles

"I took one of my husband's dirty gym shirts and kept it in a Ziploc freezer bag, unwashed. I would take it out from time to time and sniff the armpits. Yes, I did that." – Heather

"I tasted some of my husband's ashes. I was sad, and curious." – Rainee

Stop the Shame

Did you know that widows feel shame?

Did you know that widowers feel shame?

I just realized this.

As I was driving to hospice bereavement last week, it hit me like a ton of bricks.

Sometimes when I speak about Michelle, I feel shame.

And many times, I do not speak about Michelle when I want to, because I feel shame.

Yes, even me.

I know that is shocking to most of you. After all, I write about Michelle all of the time.

It's true, though. Even me, the outspoken widower from Illinois.

I feel shame.

And so many others do, too.

When the realization of this hit me, I was taken aback.

I realized that when I post about Michelle on my personal page, I sometimes cringe – because I know that there are certain people that will see my post and will think things.

He wants attention.

He still isn't over her?

Why does he talk about her so much?

He'll never find someone else if he keeps this up.

His posts make me sad.

I realized that the last time I posted something truly intense about how badly I miss Michelle on my blog, I felt shame.

The truth is, I am not blaming these people. Or their thoughts (as ignorant as they may be).

No, I am blaming myself.

And – I am blaming you – for your own shame, my fellow widows and widowers.

Only YOU have the power to stop the shame.

The ignorance of others cannot – and should not – prohibit us from loving our spouses.

The ignorance of others cannot – and should not – prohibit us from missing our spouses.

The ignorance of others cannot – and should not – prohibit us from speaking of our spouses.

The ignorance of others cannot – and should not – prohibit us from carrying their memory and love with us for the remainder of our days.

The ignorance of others cannot – and should not – prohibit us from grieving beyond the 365 day marker that has been deemed appropriate by those who know no such pain.

The ignorance of others cannot – and should not – prohibit us from grieving the way that we need to grieve, from living the way that we need to live and from loving the way that we need to love.

Let them think we do it for attention.

Let them snicker.

Let them roll their eyes.

They don't know.

They have no idea.

Their ignorance shines a bright light on their character, or lack of it.

Let it.

The truth is, while we are a community of people that can generally understand each other – EVERY situation is unique. EVERY grief is different. EVERY pain is stamped with its own custom imprint.

Judgment, even amongst each other, should be checked at the door.

Stop the shame.

If you want to talk about your deceased spouse – talk about them.

If you don't want to talk about deceased spouse – don't talk about them.

If you want to try to date again – date again.

If you don't want to try to date again – don't date again.

Stop letting others shame you into what you do, what you say and how you live.

Do what you feel is right.

Say what you want to say.

Live how you want to live.

Let me be clear, I am NOT enabling bad behavior.

No, I am not saying to drink yourself to sleep every night.

No, I am not saying to be mean or cruel to others simply because you are in pain.

No, I am not saying to quit your job and give up on life.

No, I am not saying to let the bitterness of your loss eat away at your soul.

I hope that each and every one of you can take your loss, take the immense pain from your loss, and manifest it towards a positive. Not right away, obviously, but in due time.

What I am doing, is urging you to: Stop the shame.

Stop letting the words, actions, and opinions of others dictate how you grieve.

It is your grief!

They were your spouse!

It was your future!

It is your life!

Our loves were taken from us.

Through cancer, and heart disease. Through suicide, and drug addiction. Through war, and accidents.

Our lives were turned upside-down.

Our futures were forever altered.

I am done feeling ashamed.

As much as I may type the words, I almost never say this out loud:

I MISS MY WIFE!

I MISS MY WIFE!

I MISS MY WIFE!

I want to go outside right now and I want to shout it.

Loudly.

Over and over again.

Because I have been holding it in for so long.

Out of shame.

I MISS MY WIFE!

I miss her in our youth. The teenage romance that made a young man fall madly in love with his blonde beauty. Those memories I will forever cherish.

I miss her in our past. The reuniting of soul mates after nearly a decade apart. A fairytale romance I will never forget.

I miss her in our future. 50 beautiful years together. Stolen from us in the most callous of ways.

I no longer care if people think I am weird.

I no longer care if people think my openness is embarrassing.

I no longer care what timetable people think a grieving heart should be subject to.

My shame is over.

Done.

Finished.

I don't care who judges me. Anyone who judges is too small-minded to matter.

I don't care what they say. Anything they say is too irrelevant to be taken seriously.

I don't care if the love I have for my wife makes all potential new love interests run away. Any woman who doesn't understand a heart large enough for two, lacks the depth that I require.

So, to all of my fellow widows and widowers, and to anyone else who is grieving and sometimes feels the same way, today is the day:

Stop the shame.

Warning:

You will see a commercial on TV.

This commercial will set off what the grieving refer to as a "trigger."

(As an example, commercials on cancer "trigger" me.)

You will want to throw an M&M at the TV.

Advice:

Do not throw the M&M at the TV.

Instead, eat the M&M.

And curse at the TV.

#Televisions #Are #Expensive

#And #We #Do #Not #Waste #Candy

Better Not Bitter Widower Facebook Post

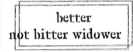

Grief is such a little bastard.

It's feeling like you want to break down on the way to the hospital to get your test done because that was the hospital that so much of your wife's cancer battle took place at.

It's once again being in awe of her strength and courage as you think about everything that she went through. It's wanting one of the nurses or doctors to ask if you are married, so that you could talk about her aloud – even if only for a second.

It's missing her a lot on the drive home, because it's warm and sunny out, and summer is right around the corner. And you won't have her to spend it with.

It's all of these things.

Mixed with pride.

That she was yours, and you were hers.

Yeah.

That's grief.

An average Monday, I think not.

I went out with a group of local widowed people.

Some I knew, some I didn't.

Towards the end of the night a conversation began with one of the widows I had never met before.

Michelle came up, so I explained some of the back story.

After we discussed Michelle, this woman made a comment to me that had me a little confused.

Was she a widow?

Or perhaps just a friend of someone who decided to tag along for the evening?

"Wait, are you a widow?" I asked.

She responded back with hesitation, telling me that she didn't know how to respond to that because they were only engaged - and not married.

"You're a widow. You're a widow," I started.

"Well, I mean unless you don't want to be a widow. You can call yourself whatever you want," I backed off a bit, realizing that she may not want to be referred to as a widow.

"I personally think you are a widow though.
A piece of paper does not measure love," I concluded.

She hesitated, without response for a moment, as she gave me a look of appreciation.

It was as if I was validating her pain, in a world that sometimes may not.

Let me be clear:

Never treat someone else's pain as less than yours simply because they do not have a marriage license.

Those who didn't make it official in time deserve all of the same love and support as the rest of us.

#piece #of #paper #or #not

Certain songs get me each and every time.

#Real #Men #Cry

*"It's been almost a decade since my husband passed away from cancer.
We were married for 28 years.*

*As time has passed, I've adjusted to life and the way it is now,
but not a day goes by where I don't think about the future that we missed out on.
He was my best friend, my confidant, and my love."*

Mama Polo

speaking about…

Papa Polo

#Michael

Dear Dad,

I told you that I was going to marry her, all the way back in 2002.

I'm sure there were multiple souls up there to greet her, I hope that one of them was you.

When I told you I was going to marry her, you responded to me clearly:

"John, she's the one."

I know I told you this in the eulogy, but it's been awhile and I realized I don't talk to you that much anymore, so just as a reminder:

I'm so honored to be your son.

Love is Eternal

Allison R. is friend that I met on Facebook.

She is also a widow.

As the one-year anniversary of her husband's passing was approaching, Allison received something.

Something special.

A text message from her 10-year-old son.

A text message that reminded Allison of the love that their family shared.

A text message that reminded Allison of the love that their family will ALWAYS share.

Here is the message that Allison received.

By the way, Flash is their dog.

Here are some facts!

F1: You are awesome

F2: I love you

F3: You love me

F4: Dad loves you

F5: Dad loves me

F6: Dad loves all of us

F7: You love all of us

F8: Flash loves all of us

F9: All these facts are true

F10: I Loooooooooove you so much!!!

Not every widowed individual had a good marriage.

Their loss is still loss.

Their pain is still pain.

We must remember this.

The (Rated G) Sex Poem

I'm not supposed to say this.

It's taboo.

But widows and widowers miss sex with our loves.

We really do.

What we would not give.

For just one more time.

Damn.

I miss her body.

Right up against mine.

The Giraffe

By Ahisha

In 2001, my husband Jeff wanted to buy me
this 4-foot wooded giraffe in a boutique in Cocoa Beach.
A fancy boutique, mind you.

I declined because it was too expensive.

Fast forward to 2014. I am barely 60 days into widowhood,
and I find myself driving 2 hours away
to Cocoa Beach to "clear my mind."

Much to my surprise, that same fancy boutique was still there.

Lo and behold, in the "CLEARANCE" area is the 4-foot giraffe.

Yes, that same giraffe that I left behind thirteen years before.

I put my hand over my mouth and immediately began hitching,
the kind of crying where you can't catch your breath or speak.
Tears, spit, and snot flying everywhere.

The owner and staff came running towards me to see what all the ruckus was about.

Through my crying fit, I paid for the giraffe and ran out of the store.

Onlookers looked at me with a mix of pity and confusion
as I wailed down the street carrying a 4-foot wooden giraffe
in the Cocoa Village Shopping district.

Do you know what I would give to see Michelle bump into a wall just one more time?

Anything.

#I'd #Give #Anything

#Daily #Occurrence

Being widowed is taking it all in.

With a deep breath.

You rest your head.

"I love you Michelle," you whisper.

To the empty side of the bed.

There's something about going to the grocery store on a holiday weekend.

It's jam packed.

With couples and families.

Happily purchasing low fat salami.

And almond milk.

It's depressing as shit.

"Well maybe you shouldn't have let the cops into the bathroom while you were pooping Michelle, I really don't know what to tell you."

- Me to her.

Kate

Meet Kate

Kate became a widow at the young age of just 29.

As though being a widow isn't hard enough, Kate did not just have herself to worry about – no, she was also left as a single mother of 4 girls.

Yes, that's right, 4 girls!

FOUR!

Girls!

Here is a Facebook post that Kate made:

 Kate

It's not about the degree. It's the accomplishment.

It's about the journey that has brought me here and finally graduating symbolizes that journey.

I am graduating at the end of this month with my Bachelors in Sociology. I know I'm in debt from it. I know my degree doesn't make a whole lot of money. When Coy died, I had to make a decision: Take a break from school or keep going. I had taken many breaks before when various obstacles prevented me from continuing and I decided that this time, I wasn't going to quit.

I owe this degree to all my loved ones who have passed away. They all saw something in me that I guess I didn't see in myself until recently. I owe it to my Mom and my Grandma, who were my role models for strength and independence. They taught me how to keep going no matter what life throws at you. I owe it to my friend, Ryan, because I promised him if I ever had the opportunity, I would go back to school. He told me he'd hold me to that. I had the opportunity and I couldn't break my promise. I owe it to my friend, Kendall, because she told me every day how intelligent I was, and she always told me I was too smart for the life I was living. She gave me the confidence to believe in myself. I owe it to my late husband, Coy, because the last thing he said before pulling the trigger was "Take care of the kids for me, Kate." I also owe it to my kids because, no matter what we go through, I have to make sure they are okay and that's what gave me the push to keep going.

Most of all, though, I owe it to myself because even through all that.... I didn't give up.

The Diploma doesn't mean much, but the journey to get it means everything.

Kate. She inspires me.

There may come a time in your journey when someone suggests to you that it is time for you to take off your wedding ring.

There may come a time in your journey when someone suggests to you that it is time for you to change your Facebook status to "Widowed."

Pay them no attention.

They know no better.

Your loss.

Your grief.

Your timeline.

Your rules.

#I #Pity #the #Fool

Michelle Marie Polo:

You made me a better man.

You've Changed

"You've changed."

Have you heard this since your loss?

Maybe you have.

Maybe you haven't.

But my guess is that you've felt it.

You've felt it about yourself.

You've felt the eyes of others judging you with those thoughts: *You've changed.*

Here are my questions: *How could you not? How could you not change? Were you supposed to remain the same? Was a deep, profound, and tragic loss not supposed to change you?*

A couple of weeks ago, I saw a meme about grief on Facebook that spoke to me; a line in it stated the following words: ***An Alteration of Your Being.***

Think about those words.

An Alteration of Your Being.

That is raw. And that is true.

You haven't just changed.

No, it's more than that.

Your very being has been altered.

Maybe it was cancer that took your loved one, or suicide. Heart disease, or a car accident.

We all have different stories. Some of us got to say good-bye. Some did not. Some of our loved ones suffered before their passing. Some did not.

Regardless of how your loss took place, regardless of the exact details of your story, one thing is almost certainly true: *You've changed.*

I know I sure have.

I went from Cloud 9, to utter despair.

I went from a man reunited with his high school sweetheart, the only woman he's ever loved, to a man desperate to save that same woman from the cancer that took over her body.

I went from truly happy, for the first time in my life, to off-the-charts bitter.
Terrified that my everything was about to be taken away.

My wife. My step-daughter.

My everything.

There were so many horrific moments during those 2 ½ years in which she fought bravely against the disease that eventually took her life.

It go to the point where there were moments, near the end, in which I begged God, with tears from the gut and desperation from the soul, to just take her already.
To take her to put her out of her misery. To take her to put me out of mine.

I had changed.

Profoundly.

And then, I changed again.

Shortly before Michelle passed away, while in hospice, I had an awakening of sorts.

I realized how blessed I was to have had Michelle in my life for as long as I did.
I realized how blessed I was to have my amazing step-daughter in my life.
I realized how blessed they both were to have me in their lives as well.

My bitterness began to fade.

I began to change for the better.

As I stand here today, nearing the one-year anniversary of the day that my wife passed away in an unexpectedly beautiful, yet obviously tragic moment, I can say that I have changed.

I have changed in dramatic ways. And I continue to change.

There are days when I am a better person. There are days when I am a worse person.

But one thing is for certain, I am surely not the same person.

My outlook on life. My goals. My desires. My heart. My soul.

None of it is quite the same.

I have changed. To my very core.

I have changed.

Often for the better. Occasionally for the worse.

I have changed.

And I'm betting you have, too.

After a deep and profound loss, I am now convinced that it is impossible to remain the same person that you once were.

So the next time someone says, "You've changed," whether it be as a compliment, a criticism, or a general observation, tell them that you know that.

Tell them that you haven't just changed, though.

Tell them what you have truly experienced *An Alteration of Your Being.*

Tell them that, for better or for worse, you'll never be the same.

Do you know what I would give to hear Michelle's laugh just one more time?

Anything.

#I'd #Give #Anything

#It #Was #Beautiful

There will be days in which you feel completely and totally overwhelmed.

There will be days in which you will feel as though simply
putting one foot in front of the other is absolutely impossible.

There will be days in which you do not think you can go on.

There will be days in which you may not want to go on.

I know.

I have been there.

We all have been there.

Breathe.

Just Breathe.

Survive First.

Exist Second.

Live 3rd

I just spent the last 45 minutes wondering what smells so bad.

It was me.

I smell so bad.

#dat #widowed #life

I Have To Go Now...

I asked everyone to leave the room. They said that we only had an hour left, and I wanted the last hour to be ours. I got into bed with her and slowly put my hand on her arm. I was scared. I remembered the day, just over 8 years ago, when I touched my dad's deceased body and it was cold. It freaked me out. I didn't want Michelle to be cold. With that memory still fresh in my head, I slowly, gently, and cautiously put my hand on her arm.

Still warm. Thank goodness.

Feeling more at ease and knowing that the clock was ticking away, I wrapped my arms around her in a full cuddle, just as I had done so many times before. All the while realizing that it would be for the very last time.

I started with the basics. I told her that I loved her, over and over again. I told her that I always had. And that I always would. I talked to her about our past, the teenage love that ended too soon and the fairytale reunion that would take place 8 years later.

I talked to her. I forgave her. I forgave myself. For anything. And everything. I talked to her about the good times that we shared before she got sick. And I talked to her about the horrific times that we experienced during her 2 1/2-year battle. I told her that I didn't know how I was going to do it, survive without her. But then, I promised her that I would I would figure it out. I promised her that I would be okay. Somehow. Someway.

For her. For me. For hers, who I loved as mine. And then, I told her about our future. The one that I know we will share. I told her that she better be waiting for me with open arms, and then I reminded her of the pinky swear that we had agreed to the week prior. That pinky swear in which we promised each other that in our next lifetime down here together, we would get our 50 years. 50 years of health, life, and love.

And then, I lay with her. And I cuddled. And I cuddled hard. And I stared. And I stared hard. And, yes, I cried. And I cried hard.

"John, it's time," they said. Family came back into the room and finished emptying out the place that had been our home for 23 life-altering days.

It was now time. Really time. To do what I had never done before. To leave her. I asked everyone to give me just one more minute by myself.

"I have to go now, Michelle. I have to go. I'm so sorry. But I have to go," I said, over and over again. "I have to go, baby. I'm so sorry, but I have to go."

Tears flowing down my cheeks, as I cried so hard I was convinced I would never be able to stop.

Leaving her. For the first time, and for the last time. All in one time. Having no choice but to go. It shattered my heart to pieces.

It devastated my soul.

Move forward.

Not

Move on.

You CAN do this.

Yes.

You can!

YES. YOU. CAN.

Grief: General Rules

1. Grief comes in waves.

2. For many, the reality of the loss endured does not hit for at least 6 months. That is when the shock wears off and when the "new normal" kicks in.

3. For children, the reality of the loss endured can take much longer to occur.

4. For a variety of reasons, year two is sometimes worse than year one.

5. There will be times in which you think that you are doing better, and then a major setback will occur.   This is normal. This is to be expected.

6. Grief comes in waves.

7. You are not crazy. You are grieving. There is a difference.

8. Grief is both predictable and unpredictable.

9. Expect the unexpected. From grief. From yourself. From others.

10. Grief comes in waves.

11. There is no timeline for grief.
    Anyone who tries to tell you that there is does not know what they are talking about.

12. *#Ignore #Them*

From wanting to die.

To determined to live.

You made that happen.

You refused to let me give in.

"No, John. You are not going to give up.
You will make it through this.
I know that you can."

It's because of you, Michelle,
that even in the most hopeless of times,
I am, somehow, a hopeful man.

That's me.

People ask why I don't smile.

I do.

They just don't see.

They don't see how I smile with my eyes.

My eyes that do that and so much more.

My eyes, they have seen happiness.

And they have seen horror.

My eyes see flashbacks, to the memories that we shared.

They envision the future that was stolen from us and they wonder what will be.

An inner battle. Between hopeful and scared.

But when the raw emotions die down.

And I take a deep breath.

My eyes smile.

That she was mine. And I am hers.

In life. And. In death.

This is a bathroom selfie.

Yes.

I put a bathroom selfie in my book.

Why?

Because my name is John Polo.

#and #i #am #a #freak

The one-year benchmark is COMPLETE crap.

**Those who think it takes 365 days to heal,
have likely have never lost a piece of their heart.**

Better Not Bitter Widower Facebook Post

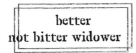

If Michelle were still alive, we would still be married. We would still be happy. We would still be in love.

Now do you understand why fifteen months has not erased my pain?

Now do you understand why time does not actually heal all wounds?

It's because their absence is felt in everything that we do.

It is felt in every moment. It is felt every day.

Grief does not end.

Yes, it changes.

Yes, it gets easier in some ways.

But no, it does NOT end.

Any person who does not understand such a thing is not worth your time,
or attention.

#They #Don't #Know

Scott

Meet Scott

"Asher's Daddy."

That is what Scott's Facebook profile says.

Yes. He sure is.

Scott lost his amazing wife, Danissa, to cancer.

While she may not be here with them in the physical form, I know she is looking down on them.

Smiling, and beaming with pride.

Here is a Facebook Post that Scott made:

 Scott

Asher is my angel.

Anyone who knows me knows this to be true. Like his mother, Danissa, I knew I loved him the moment I met him.

For years, I loved Danissa so strongly that I was sure I could see our unborn child in her eyes. Now, I see her in his big, beautiful, brown eyes and infectious smile each day. It doesn't seem fair that I would be raising him without her, because I know he is missing the best half of his creation. A creation made from true, unconditional love. Of course, it wasn't always easy, but somehow we made it work, and from that union came the child who brings me to tears multiple times each day just by looking at him and feeling the strongest love I have ever felt. To see his smile, to hear his laugh, to watch how he loves everything and everyone around him - it's hard not see Danissa.

He has been the blood that has pumped through my body these 4 years since Danissa died, the motivation to go on.

Scott. He inspires me.

I talk to Michelle all of the time.

Yes.

All of the time.

Sometimes, I tell her that I love her. And that I miss her.

Sometimes, I tell her that I am mad at her. For leaving me.

Sometimes, I talk to her dirty. Because I miss that booty.

#Damn

#She #Was #So #Good #Looking

#No #Shame #in #My #Widower #Game

Sneak Peek of My Upcoming Book

My Michelle

That evening, I took out my electric razor and shaved Michelle's head over the bathroom sink. I went extremely slow, and I tried to be as gentle as possible as I used my right hand to cut her hair and my left hand to rub her back in an attempt to comfort her. There's something about shaving the head of your sick, depleted, fragile, and now nearly-bald wife that makes you love her more than you have ever loved her before. That's one thing about watching someone you love battle cancer with such strength, dignity, kindness, and grace. You realize each day that you love them more than you loved them the day before, something that you thought was not even humanly possible.

"I think you should keep it like this. You look awesome. You rock that shit," I proclaimed honestly.

She did look awesome and she did rock that shit.

She was in effect bald, but we decided to keep it as a short buzz cut for the time being since she looked so good like that, even knowing that this new hairdo would be short-lived as the rest of her golden locks would soon be making a departure.

PSA:

Shut. Up.

"Everything Happens for a Reason."

Yes, They Did! – Take 2

"My husband's ashes were in a box. I taped a picture of him to the box and he and I went to Hooters together. I made him a plate, placed it on the box, and we had dinner together. People may have thought I was weird, but I just wanted to have dinner with my husband again. So their judgment didn't matter." – Karen

"Ever since she passed away I use the exact brand of deodorant that my wife used to use. I may smell like a lady, but at least I smell like my lady. It brings me comfort." – Andy

"I found an old Chap-Stick of my husband's. I was giddy when I found it. Every day, I would apply just a tiny bit until it ran out. It was like I was getting one small kiss from him each time I used it." – Cheryl

"The day after my wife's funeral, our daughter headed back to college. I was home, all by myself, for the first time in 22 years. I went to our dresser and emptied out every pair of underwear (bras and panties) that my wife had. I threw them all on the bed. For 2 weeks, I slept in the bed like that, surrounded by all of her underwear. Our daughter ended up coming home a week early to surprise me and caught me taking a nap in the bed, with all of her mother's underwear. Needless to say, she was traumatized." – Joseph

(Don't) Call me Lucky

You are lucky. You got to say good-bye.

You are lucky. You didn't have to watch them die.

No.

No.

No.

And, one more time for good measure: NO!

I lost my wife to cancer. To one of the most rare and aggressive cancers known to man.

A cancer so rare that only one person a year in the world gets what she had.

For 2 ½ years, I watched her suffer.

I watched her suffer physically.
The images of her pain embedded into my brain for the rest of time.

I watched her suffer mentally.
The knowledge that she was battling an aggressive beast inside of her that was not to be beaten.

I watched her suffer emotionally.
The realization of what was to come and who she would be leaving behind.

I am lucky?

No. I am not lucky.

The horror of a 2 ½-year cancer battle from Hell does not make me lucky.

Fact: There is nothing lucky about watching someone you love die a slow and painful death.

You know who else is not lucky?

You.

The person who lost your love suddenly.

The person who lost your love from a heart attack. Or a car accident.

The person who lost your love from a murder. Or a war.

True, you may not have watched them suffer.

True, their pain may not have been as prolonged.

That does not make you lucky.

Not in any way. Shape. Or form.

Fact: There is nothing lucky about losing someone you love suddenly, and without warning.

You had no time to prepare. No chance to say good-bye.

You had no chance to say everything one last time.

I am not saying that all loss is equal. I am actually saying the exact opposite.

Each and every loss is unique.

Each and every pain its own.

As the exact circumstances of each situation and passing are different, there are undoubtedly some losses that are more tragic than others.

The truth, though, is this:
When you lose someone you love dearly, 'Lucky' is not a word that you EVER want to hear.

Don't tell me that I am lucky because I got to say good-bye.

Don't tell them that they are lucky because they did not have to watch them die.

Save that word.

For the healthy. For the living. For the carefree.

Lucky?

We only wish that we could be.

Widow: The Weapon

By Cheryl B.

As I was saying, I am now a widow.
I don't know that I'm a good widow.
What is a good widow anyway?

For the first few months in, I didn't even want to be called a widow.

I used the word only as a weapon.

"I'm a widow, so leave me the Hell alone."

"Why are you bothering me with your dumb questions?
Don't you know I'm a widow?"

"My husband died! Leave me alone."

"Oh, you're calling for my husband? Well, he's not here, he died and I'm his widow."

"I don't feel like it today. I'm widowed and I'm dealing with feeling bad."

"Could you just get out of my way?
I'm a widow and I just want to do what I came to do and leave."

"Can you stop talking? I am a widow and I just don't want to hear it."

"How am I?
I'm a fucking widow.
How do you think I am?"

Hugs.

I know.

I miss them too.

#So #Damn #Much

Thank YOU!

To all those who have allowed me to share their words in this book.

Your bravery will inspire others.

A number of my contributors have their own blogs, books or small businesses

Alicia
Blogger
Find her on Facebook @ Brave for Dave and Alicia

Ben
Blogger
www.thechoppywater.com

Cecilia
Blogger & Photographer
www.suitcaseofgrief.wordpress.com
www.ceciliamarieportraiture.com
www.deleazoboudoir.com

Emily Ann
Blogger
www.readysetgrieve.wordpress.com
Find her on Facebook @ Read, Set, Grieve?

Cheryl B.

Blogger

www.thinkabouttellingmystory.wordpress.com

Find her on Facebbok @ Widowness and Light

Michelle Miller

Author & Blogger

www.mouthymichellesmusings.com

Kerry

Blogger

www.youngwidowedanddating.com

Sabra Robinson

Author/Blogger/Podcaster

www.blackwomenwidowsempowered.com

(Her new book will feature Cheryl B., Kerry and LaTisha)

Susan

Author & Social Worker

www.a2zhealingtoolbox.com

Find her on Facebook @ A2Z Healing Toolbox

Kerry

Meet Kerry

Kerry lost her husband to malaria. She was just 32 years old when he passed away.

As she found herself a young widow, Kerry had a decision to make.

It was no easy journey, but Kerry choose hope.

Today, Kerry helps countless people with her blog and her widowed Facebook group.

She is even a blogger for the Huffington Post – I can't even get on the Huffington Post!

She's just so cool.

Here is a Facebook post that Kerry made:

 Kerry

I don't always share my joys because, quite honestly, I struggle with having such immense joy in my life. At times, I feel like this joy betrays my husband's memory.

I am 5 years into widowhood and I never imagined my life would ever get back to pure, unadulterated joy.

I am visiting my in-laws. I am in the same house where we had so many wonderful memories. It is where we dreamed of what our children would be like, what our future would look like.

When I got the call that he was unexpectedly gone, sitting alone in the church parking lot, I felt broken, shattered into a million pieces that would never be made whole.

But today, I am here. Lying in the room next to the kitchen that is filled with so many memories of him.

Lying next to my daughter that I chose to have after his death, and I am happy.

I told my MIL that I struggle with this joy.

She looked me in the face and said, "You were hurt and had a devastating blow. Don't you think you deserve this joy? Why would you fight what God has blessed you with? You have something that money can't buy. Appreciate it!"

I DESERVE THIS JOY (and so do you!).

If you don't have it yet, it is coming, hang on!

Kerry. She inspires me.

I miss Michelle more as time passes.

Not less.

Better Not Bitter Widower Facebook Post

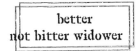

Yes, grief changes.

Yes, grief itself gets easier.

No, grief does not end.

BUT…

Something interesting happens that I have felt for the last couple of months now, but could not quite explain, until this very moment.

As the full-out meltdowns seem to become a thing of the past, and the gut-wrenching tears become less frequent, there is one thing that becomes more profound:

Their absence.

I miss Michelle more today than ever before.

Does that mean that I am grieving harder than ever before?

Absolutely not.

Grief has changed.

Grief has lessened.

Grief has eased.

BUT…

The longing for my wife, the missing of her physical presence, and the absence of her in everything that we do, has become more profound.

We ache for their hand. To hold it just one more time.

We ache for their lips. For just one more kiss.

We ache for their smile. To see it for even just a second, would bring us the ultimate bliss.

That is why we aren't over it yet.

That is why we NEVER get over it.

The longer that we go without them, the more that we miss them.

Baby, I Miss You in the Sun

I miss you in the sun.

The truth is, obviously, that I miss you every day.

Even when it's dark. Even when it's grey.

There is something about the sun, though.

That makes me miss you that much more.

The pain it causes.

It hurts me to my core.

I fell for you in the sun.

The spring of 2002. That is when I first noticed you.

The summer of that same year,

I finally got the courage to ask you to be mine.

What a summer it was.

It's when we fell in love together for the very first time.

Short shorts.

Sexy hips.

Soft lips.

You could turn me into a blubbering idiot.

With a just simple kiss.

I fell so madly in love with your mind, your body, and your soul.

Our love was true.

But our youth took its toll.

It wasn't meant to be.

It didn't last.

John and Michelle

Became a thing of the past.

But then one day, out of the blue,

I received an e-mail.

From Michelle.

After 8 years.

It was you.

The feelings came rushing back.

In an instance.

Clearly never gone.

Despite the time. Despite the distance.

The sun was there when you called me again for the first time.

You butt-dialed me.

Just like you use to do.

Way back. When you were mine.

It was my birthday.

July twenty-one.

What a present to receive.

An accidental phone call.

It was you.

It was the one.

The love was back.

The love was grand.

You know what else happened in the sun, Michelle?

Yes.

I asked you for your hand.

For the rest of my days, I will remember that night.

You were so surprised.

It all felt just so right.

50 beautiful years together.

That is what it was supposed to be.

Little did we know of the future that we would so unluckily see.

Your diagnosis.

On a warm sunny day.

From happiness, to Hell on Earth.

This wasn't supposed to be the way.

I miss you in the sun.

For all of the moments that we had.

Our summer love. Our reunion. Our grand plan.

That magical night that I asked you for your hand.

I miss you in the sun.

For the future moments that we will miss.

I would give anything, Michelle.

For just one more summer kiss.

Excerpt from Better Not Bitter Widower Blog

"Hospice: The Gift We Never Wanted to Receive"

I think about telling Michelle. Over and over again. Because each time that she would wake up in the hospital bed, she would forget what I had told her a few hours prior. And she would demand to know what was going on. And I would have to tell her again that she was going to die. And that she was going to die very soon.

The most heartbreaking tears that you can ever imagine. Over and over again.

Because, apparently, living that experience once wasn't enough pain for us to endure.

SUPERMAN

There are days that I feel like him.

Like I can conquer the world.

Like I can accomplish anything.

And then, there are other days.

Other days.

Days of deep grief.

Days of intense pain.

Days where progress seems impossible.

A Cheesy Poem

(Because I Am Cheesy)

Michelle would call me a lady.

#Perhaps #I #Am

Michelle would call me an idiot.

#No #Doubt #That's #True

Michelle knew just how to love me.

And

I knew just how to love her too.

In sickness and in health...

Widowed. Rants, Raves and *Randoms*

Sneak Peek of My Upcoming Book

My Michelle

One of the last things that Michelle said to me while she was coherent was on a Monday night, a couple of weeks before she passed, as we laid together, holding hands in her bed at hospice.

"John, you didn't lie to me," she said.

I asked her what she meant by that.

"You didn't lie, you told me till death do us part, and you didn't lie." she responded.

"You're right, Michelle. I didn't lie. I've loved you forever and I always will." I whispered back.

Then we pinky swore, promising each other that in our next life down here together, we will get our 50 years.

50 years of health.

50 years of happiness.

50 years of love.

**Save a few articles of your late spouse's clothing
and have items made out of them.**

Ideas for items include: Pillows, blankets, and stuffed animals.

For children and adults alike, this can be an incredible gift of comfort and love.

I don't really know who I have become since Michelle passed away but, apparently, it's the type of guy who writes poetry while he thugs out to 2Pac.

#multi #layered

#poet

#didn't #know #it

We can sit here and ask "why?"

Why Michelle?

Of all the people this tragedy could have hit, why did cancer have to take Michelle?

Why such a beautiful soul?

Why now, just after we both found our way back to each other and found
the happiness we had been searching for all of our lives?

None of us know, nor will we ever.

I often questioned why God even brought us back together to just rip us apart.

I asked this until my sister asked me a question:

"Would you rather have never gotten back together
and found out years later that she had died of this terrible disease?"

That question changed me.

I think Michelle needed me.

I think she needed my unconditional love, my support, my care.

I think I needed Michelle.

Her love, her warm touch, her smile, her perspective on life.

She showed me what a beautiful life could be, what true strength is,
what having true character and class really means.

We showed each other, in our short time together,
that we both were deserving of true, unconditional love.

We showed each other the life that we had both always dreamed of.

Sneak Peek of My Upcoming Book

My Michelle

I read it to her. I have no idea how, but I did it. I couldn't stop crying. They say that they can hear you, and even if that is true, the fact that I was crying so hard means, realistically, she probably couldn't understand much of what I was saying anyway.

I read her the eulogy.

I wanted her to hear it before anyone else.

I told her that I hoped it made her proud, and then I cried some more.

You must be your own advocate during this process.

Speak up.

If you want to say your spouse "passed away,"
then say they "passed away."

If you want to say your spouse "died,"
then say they "died."

#Say #What #You #Want #To #Say

They Say...

*"I'm coming up on 2 years since my life was shattered by Susan's passing.
I remember hearing people in grief support meetings saying how they thought it got harder
after the first year. I refused to believe it. Now I understand what they meant.
It's not the grief or the daily mourning that gets harder. That becomes a part of you.
It's the intolerance of others around you that becomes the true test of your spirit." – Ben*

*"The worst part of being a suicide widow is knowing that my husband chose to stop living.
He chose to make me a widow. He chose to leave our children fatherless.
The vulnerability of widowhood is exacerbated by his having a choice in dying;
it's born from knowing that he could have made the choice to stay alive.
And it's that awful realization which broke me. He was ill with an affliction that most
couldn't necessarily see. Even still, he could have chosen differently." – Amber*

*"I told my girls that Daddy is in everything. The grass, the clouds, the sky.
He is in the birds that fly. He is around us every moment of our lives." – Kate*

*"He died of an overdose and, because of that, the regular compassion that most receive
was not there. To the world, he wasn't worth missing. He wasn't a person.
He wasn't a father, a husband, or a son.
To the world, he was just a junky, and his life didn't matter.
That's what he was to the world. But to us, he was everything.
Cory was our hero, and our best friend. He still is, and he always will be." – Emily*

Sneak Peek of My Upcoming Book

My Michelle

It was supposed to be our dance, our moment in time, the ending to a fairytale romance and the beginning of 50 beautiful years of happiness and joy.

I imagined this knowing that it was a dream. A dream that could no longer come true. I read the words that I had written for my beautiful wife, somehow managing to only choke up and not completely fall apart.

I read and people listened.

I honored her, as she deserved to be honored.

"Do not ever allow yourself to be bullied out of grief.

You are allowed to break."

– Sabra Robinson

"We don't survive it. We let it kill the old us and then we rebuild."

– Michelle Miller

John,

What does one say to you?

**No words can bring her back. No words make it easier.
Does one really find "comfort" with words?**

This is what I know:

You swept Michelle off her feet not once, but twice.

**The second time you thought you needed her more –
it turned out she needed you more.**

**What you did for her during her fight
was something I have never seen before.**

**The way you were there for her –
I have never witnessed before.**

**Your happily-ever-after was taken away 50 years too early;
however, you were her Prince Charming to the end.**

Thank you for giving her the true love she deserved.

- Lisa

"I believe that God made you to love her."

- Julie

Allison

This is Allison.

This is Allison getting her hair did on her Wedding Anniversary.

This is widowhood.

I Am Not Supposed to Be Here.

I AM NOT SUPPOSED TO BE HERE.

My mind was made up.

It was not a matter of if I would join Michelle.

It was only a matter of how I would join Michelle.

I fell madly in love with her at the age of 18.

One year together, she broke my heart.

5 years together as adults. Death did us part.

Watching her get sick. Watching her die.

The anger. The bitterness. The sadness. The distress.

The fear of losing my entire family. It was too much to bear.

The realization that she would not be cured. The unbelievable pain endured.

The physical pain and agony that she went through.

I tried so hard to save her. In the end, there was nothing that I could do.

I have something that I must confess.

I am deeply ashamed of this, but I have told you so much already, I might as well tell you the rest.

I told her about my plan.

I wish that I could say it was simply a moment of distress.

That I put on a brave face for her, let her battle the disease, and I handled the rest.

The truth though is, that is not how it occurred.

I failed my wife. In the truest sense of the word.

Now, don't get me wrong. I took damn good care of my wife.

I took care of all her medical needs. Became her caregiver. Searched the world for a cure.

Never left her side.

I showed her that my love was pure.

When she had her moments of sadness and despair, I was strong. I was there.

We made a great team in that way.

The perfect pair.

But still. I failed her.

In a very significant way.

For that is a regret that I still carry with me to this day.

I was going to join her.

That was the plan.

Consumed by sadness and bitterness, my life was going to be taken by my own hand.

My mind destroyed. My heart broken. My soul so angry.

And then, I was awakened.

In a moment, my bitterness gone.

Appreciation, hope and strength found.

I discovered my purpose.

My soul peaceful. My mind sound.

We were brought together again for a reason.

It is very clear to me now.

The path forward. I finally see how.

I got to call Michelle my wife.

Being her husband and caring for her, one of the greatest honors of my life.

My role now is to be the best man that I can be.

To write, to share, to try and help others see.

I am here to be "Johnny Poo," which is what my other love so graciously calls me.

Here to make sure that she never, ever forgets her incredible Mommy.

I AM SUPPOSED TO BE HERE.

It was not my time.

The reunion of John and Michelle will have to wait.

Michelle, please tell Etta that I said that I am sorry, but I've found myself -
and I'm going to be a little late.

How to follow, or work with, John:

For access to my social media pages, books, journals, 1-on-1 coaching, courses, groups, events and more check out my website

@ www.betternotbitterwidower.com

"Your books. Your coaching. YOU!! You've changed my life."
– Deanna

Terminal cancer,
and still –

she
smiled.

Made in the USA
Columbia, SC
24 July 2023

20845079R00087